SERIE d'ECRITURE
No. 21

Isabelle Baladine Howald

SECRET OF BREATH

translated from the French
by Eléna Rivera

Burning Deck/Anyart, Providence

SERIE d'ECRITURE is an annual of current French writing in English translation. The first five issues were published by SPECTACULAR DISEASES, which continues to be a source for European distribution and subscription. Since No. 6, the publisher has been Burning Deck in Providence, RI.
Editor: Rosmarie Waldrop

Individual copies $14. Subscription for 2 issues: $24.
Supplements: $8

Distributors:
Small Press Distribution, 1341 Seventh St,. Berkeley CA 94710
1-800/869-7553; orders@spdbooks.org
Spectacular Diseases, c/o Paul Green, 83b London Rd., Peterborough, Cambs. PE2 9BS
H Press, www.hpress.no
US subscriptions: Burning Deck, 71 Elmgrove Ave., Providence RI 02906

Burning Deck Press is the Literature Program of ANYART: CONTEMPORARY ARTS CENTER, a tax-exempt (501c3), non-profit organization.

Sections of this translation were first published in *Circumference: Poetry in Translation*.
The translator wishes to thank Rosmarie Waldrop, Russell Switzer and Denise Newman for their invaluable help and thoughtful suggestions.

Cover by Keith Waldrop

Thanks to Gérard Haller, with deep regard.

"Gebirge: Schwärze, Schweigen und Schnee."

— Georg Trakl

Everything, deprived of everything.

Fleeing as quickly as possible, leaving clothing, furniture,
closet doors open, chairs overturned,
no matter.

Running,
books piled up, child carried, and one left behind in the ground,
race toward the north, in winter.

From the bottom toward the bottom.

From sundown to sundown.
From blackness toward blackness.

Every line of the day dissolved.

Driving quickly as always, and my eyes face the mountains as always.
When all the customs are lifted, the inspectors gone, there's always one that ends up staying behind to frisk and brainwash: "Halt! Stop! Don't tell anymore tales!"

Severed.
Ancient welts that nothing has diminished
and which rising,

swerve.

That which has always been
separates us
all.

"Dazzled and then nothing," he told me after having fallen.

Who will have decided this severing.

The body huddled near the window,
as if emptied.
The arms fall back, letting go.
Didn't understand anything, didn't know what this body
    was doing here,
didn't remember.

Trees, thatches, stones, likewise burned.

Without force, without possible diversion.
Over there Terre de Sienne, his land
yet far from here.

When coming from the mountains to see nothing between the firs,
even in summer,
just a few gaps, brief and somber.

The names of the ancestors summoned.

They don't respond.

It's a method of forgetting.

No longer pushing away the obsession.

Seeking. Like an exploration, slow, diligent, desperate, looks, faces, bodies.

Repeating in front of this face and this body:
"There is something, there is something."

As if that could steer me clear of being surprised, it will come, it will come anyway despite all the detours, all of the country roads and the circling, all of the watch towers, all the cross-roads, the secrecy, the vigils, the sentries, the war paint and the poor schemes, all the spotlights turned on all night, the sub-marines, the coast guards, the sniffer planes and the love of fog.

What I love is not seeing, it's the effort of seeing:

waiting non-stop for it to disappear,
beyond a sign, beyond a cry,
no formula and no sound.

To diminish, to fade,

to die.

To veil myself from his eyes.

And for me, how will it be.

This is the first time that I know who will die this year.

That which is found again, later,
tremors
— one can't expect anything else.

The bodies have aged,
so many things have foundered,
one doesn't see anymore.

Wanting still to read, discriminate, understand,
they make an effort to keep from falling,
holding each other upright:

"It's the first time that we touch each other," you tell me; later you asked me not to speak to them about it.

How will it be afterwards, how will I stay upright, how
will I do without the intonations,
how to continue.

More fear than any child in the world in the worst of fears.

Never to be able to say more,
even to the one that knows all about it,
try, try to talk.

And when one undresses,
and when one walks,
and when the bodies clash,

the throbbing, the rhythm,
the only one.

"Leave me, now," he tells me.

Why do anything,
the speed of it all,
staying upright, half dead,

and the eye that sees nothing?

In this light, the day's outcome,
the heat, the cold, the mouths
cease.

In three beats the name comes down,

and then soon after the breaths,
no more movement, barely a kiss,

to touch, come.

Look without astonishment — I am here,
to uphold what matters to us,
to lift up what falters,
to hold back what yields.

Little daylight, too much darkness,
to know of what to speak,
renounce,

and just the skin
brought to the lips in thought,
your hand holding back my hair.

Falling against the old gravel,
not hear save a few notes
(used to have a light touch). Piano, 1979.

So little space left, an opening;
hard to catch sight of.

It will come, I know it, we know it:

He will die, you will die, I will die.

We knew where the terror was,
and we said nothing,
we accepted it.

But we forgot in the name of what,
of whom.

To this — to write —, compelled, silent:

He kept on asking for paper.

Breathing every other time,
with the other mouth's breath

— not even a kiss, I don't even kiss you anymore, as if
sealed by the distance

no longer moves, the one
no longer moves, the other.

The only response, if it occurs,
won't be heard.

Imagine this as that which never ceased to wake us,
the piercing whistle, or this spasm, this twitch,
on falling asleep.

"Cover mine with yours, again,
again.
— I don't understand what you're saying.
— It's like before, already you didn't understand anything."

Something faltered, where, how, why, something previous to
everything else perhaps.

Am I to understand that we will never truly speak to each other again.

That it is finished, the talking of everything and of nothing, finished talking of things that are terrible, that I can only attempt to clear myself a path, being so afraid of losing him, scratched by the foliage, answering more or less, staying on a parallel path, neither at the same speed nor with the hope of our crossing.

That I will have to pretend, that there will never be the least bit of help, that I will approach at the speed of light the promise made:

"Be quick" (words on a page)

Not to know,
to think at the edge of oblivion,

seated in the snow,
it too inaccessible,
and asking:

but what, and of whom.

What is this, tears?
Tell me, is it you who cries?

A little before leaving, knowing that I would never see him again,
I wiped a tear from his cheek; though he wasn't crying.
She was alone and he asleep, and something was crying.

I write to move more quickly than the pain.

To date, war everywhere,
the fields, the forests of birch trees,
the wind, the grass, the low light,

the earth is plundered and the bodies abandoned.
They changed the names of countries,
they no longer even know from what. Or of whom they speak,

and here we are at these gaping borders.

All of the East, mountains, fields and steppes enclosed in metal and gutted. Mitteleuropa dreams of the infinite and knows only loss and the absence of names.

This can scarcely be written, or not at all,
nevertheless we write it,

knowing ourselves beyond repair.

We will not be reunited:

No sharing to that.

Up until the early hours waiting
for the farewells to take place,

light the lamps,
though the light keeps going out,

that which lights the way, that which hides it,
is not visible.

"It's nothing," he says several times,
doubled over, prostrate,
his hands caught in mine.

It's nothing that approaches.

I must leave you. I must not die with you.

Shadows have stretched you.
Your head on my chest,
everything heavy on your shoulders,

Dancing, shapeless, the shadows,
bearing his death with me.

You know, what approaches
is already here. It was already here.

I am lost in your smile,
of course (my angel) I remember,
that's all I do, all my life.

I brush the abyss continuously and construct, at full speed, steps, ramps, frameworks, walls, posts, to hold onto while everything collapses from all sides. Though I don't drive, I'm speeding at 200 kilometers per hour to keep in front of this groundswell.

We still laugh sometimes, as if nothing serious were happening;
afterwards it's worse.

Wrapped around himself,
his thin arms crossed at the level of his wrist
and in front of his face which he protects this way
— death touches the figure —
like praying backwards,
falling asleep suddenly,
or reopening eyes that don't seem to see.

The head, thrown back, that same ashen blond,
hair tangled, that I keep tidying tirelessly.

Soon:

The date that only to itself is known will however be revealed to me, and from this night, from this dream on, I will not live anymore (he will not read this text).

To you only will I say, as often when I call to you in the same place, near the old walls, on a quiet street: "I dreamed the date." "Prognosis: eighteen more days." Eighteen days later, he was buried in the ground, the last word pronounced was: "ashes."

To write alone for nothing and no one, here is what's left.

I won't have time to see it coming, it will always be too late.

I look, but no, nothing is happening, it's in me the sounds, the screams and howls, that is to say, warnings of danger.

The tires scream as though someone were insane with pain but no one moves, the armored cars carrying valuables pass by accompanied by police cars their sirens howling, no one blinks an eye, it's inside me when it seems as if it's outside, it's inside me when there's nothing going on outside, the telephone rings and I run for it but no it isn't ringing, it's inside me when it seems outside, it's inside me when there's nothing going on outside.

I murmur while he sleeps: "If you want, you can leave."

Always: "I don't know,"
ignorant of what it's all about
— to some extent all death has already started.

Not to recognize this noise,
or this step, or a friction, a sliding,
or from where it comes.

Perhaps there isn't any noise.

NOTE:

P. 19 "sniffer planes:" The term *avions renifleurs* refers to a scandal that occured in France in 1976, when the French Government spent 800 million Francs for planes to sniff out oil.

BIOGRAPHICAL NOTE:

Isabelle Baladine Howald lives and works in Strasbourg, France, where she studied philosophy and now directs the "Philosophical and Literary Encounters" of the Librairie Kléber. From 1980 to 1982 she edited the literary journal *ANIMA* (Jacques Brémond publishers). Her most recent books beside the present *Secret des souffles* are *Nuit d'amour un livre* and *Les noms, très bas,* published by éditions A Passage, as well as *Les Etats de la demolition* (éditions Jacques Brémond). Three books are forthcoming: *La séparation de l'âme et du corps, Hantômes* (after Mallarmé), and *L'origine des larmes.*

Howald's "Stele for Lenz" has appeared in English, in Keith Waldrop's translation, in *Série d'Ecriture No. 7* and *One Score More: The Second 20 Years of Burning Deck* (Providence: Burning Deck, 2002).

Eléna Rivera was born in Mexico City and spent her childhood, to the age of thirteen, in Paris. She is the author of *Mistakes, Accidents and a Want of Liberty* (Barque Press, 2006) and *Suggestions at Every Turn* (Seeing Eye Books, 2005). Translations can be found in *Chicago Review* and *Circumference: Poetry in Translation.* She was recently awarded the 2007 Witter Bynner Poetry Translator Residency at the Santa Fe Art Institute.